U.S. CUSTOMS AND BORDER PROTECTION

USE OF FORCE REVIEW: CASES AND POLICIES

February 2013

Conducted by

The Police Executive Research Forum
1120 Connecticut Ave, NW, #930
Washington DC 20036

Introduction

The Police Executive Research Forum (PERF) was commissioned by U.S. Customs and Border Protection (CBP) to conduct a review of the Use of Force by CBP officers and agents. This review included all CBP use of deadly force events from January 2010 through October 2012 and CBP use of force policies, equipment, tactics, and training. Sources of information were government-furnished information, equipment and materials and CBP policy documents.

PERF reviewed Customs and Border Protection Use of Force Policies and 67 case files related to Customs and Border Protection agents' use of deadly force. Case files were sorted in general categories to include: firearm response to subjects armed with firearms; firearm response to rocks thrown on land; firearm response to rocks thrown on water; firearms use against vehicles; and other firearm cases.

Policies included the "Use of Force Policy Handbook" and the following ten directives:

- 4510-020C: U.S. Customs and Border Protection Body Armor Policy
- 4510-026b: Controlled Tire Deflation Device Directive
- 4510-029: Pepperball Launching System (PLS) Policy
- 4510-029a: Use of Electronic Control Devices
- 4510-031: FN303 Less Lethal Launcher System Policy
- 4510-032: Less Lethal Specialty Impact – Chemical Munitions Policy
- 4510-033: Use of Air Disabling Fire Policy
- 4510-034: CBP Use Of Force Steering Committee (UFSC)
- 4510-035: Foreign Attaché Firearms Directive
- 5290-012a: CBP Use Of Force Incident Review Program

The case reviews raise a number of concerns, especially with regard to shots fired at vehicles and shots fired at subjects throwing rocks and other objects at agents. Improvements are also recommended in initial reporting, investigation, incident review, weapons, personal protective equipment, and training. Recommendations for changes in policies flow from these case reviews.

Two policy and practice areas especially need significant change. First, officers/agents should be prohibited from shooting at vehicles unless vehicle occupants are attempting to use deadly force--other than the vehicle--against the agent. Training and tactics should focus on avoiding positions that put agents in the path of a vehicle and getting out of the way of moving vehicles.

Second, officers/agents should be prohibited from using deadly force against subjects throwing objects not capable of causing serious physical injury or death to them. Officers/agents should be trained to specific situations and scenarios that involve subjects throwing such objects. The training should emphasize pre-deployment strategies, the use of cover and concealment, maintaining safe distances, equipping vehicles and boats with protective cages and/or screening, de-escalation strategies, and where reasonable the use of less-lethal devices.

Because these changes are significant departures from current practice CBP will need to craft an implementation strategy for re-orientation and training before new policies go into effect. Consideration should be give to assembling an expert panel to interact with members of CBP from all levels of the organization for discussion about the transition to the new policies and practices.

There are several areas where CBP is engaged in best policing practices. Firearms qualification occurs four times a year. According to policy, exemptions are limited. This practice is critical given the environment in which CBP officers/agents work.

In addition, CBP is to be commended for implementing a new incident mapping software program. This system allows examination of use of force and other incidents at both a highly detailed level and at a more macro level. This system will provide graphic support for leaders to spot trends and make strategic changes.

CBP also has produced a very useful quick-reference guide "Documenting the Use of Force." Policy changes restricting the use of deadly force against vehicles and rock throwers should be incorporated into the guide.

Case Reviews and Observations

PERF reviewed Border Patrol Use of Force Policies and 67 case files related to Border Patrol agents' use of deadly force. Case files were sorted in general categories to include: firearm response to armed suspect actions; firearm response to rocks thrown at agents on land; firearm response to rocks thrown at agents on water; firearms use against vehicles; and "other."

Case reviews were limited to assessments from the information supplied to PERF. Some case files were incomplete and were missing information. *Case summaries were reviewed to discover overall trends and patterns. The scope of the study asked for general case reviews, but not judgments on individual cases.*

Overall Observations and Recommendations:

- Initial Reporting:

  It is believed that rock throwing incidents along the border are likely very frequent; however, only serious cases where deadly force is used are routinely officially reported. One of the causes for this laxity of reporting is believed to be the complexity of report requirements in cases of "Assaults on Federal Officers."

  Recommendation: CBP policy and practice should be changed to require at least an abbreviated report in all cases of attempted assaults against agents. Accurate reporting of all incidents of attempted assaults by rocks or other means is important in order to understand the gravity of the threat and put the threat in perspective for the public and policy makers on both sides of the border.

- Investigations:

  Recommendation: All uses of deadly force should be thoroughly investigated whether injuries occur or not. Lack of diligence was observed in some investigations. It is recognized that the investigation of cases involving an international border can be limited by jurisdictional cooperation, witness availability, and access to the incident scenes. However, it is important that, to the extent possible, a full investigation be conducted of each discharge of deadly force by CBP officers/agents. Based on the somewhat limited records that were provided, it appears that CBP is not as diligent with follow up investigation and evaluations of cases where shots were fired and injuries were not confirmed. This "no harm - no foul" practice can lead to tacit approval of bad practices.

- Incident Reviews:

  Recommendation: It is not clear that CBP consistently and thoroughly reviews all use of deadly force incidents. Individual cases should be uniformly judged by a single internal process that considers comments from a shooting review board made up of internal subject matter experts who look at policy, agent safety, training, and equipment issues pertaining to each case. The shooting review process should be standardized as part of the Use of Force Incident Review Program described in directive 5290-012A. Additionally, strategic analysis of case trends should be performed on a regular basis. Such analysis may spot trends that suggest actions that require policy or equipment changes, collaboration within or outside of CBP, or problem solving. Information to support such actions is becoming increasingly available. CBP is to be commended for implementing a new incident mapping and analysis software program. This system will provide decision/analytic support for leaders to spot trends and make strategic changes.

- Weapons:

  Border protection along the U.S./Mexico Border is a unique and hazardous assignment. Frequent and dangerous rock attacks and other attacks on agents take place when agents are patrolling or making arrests near the border. In many cases, agents must effect drug seizures and arrests under threat of such attacks. For example, when drug smugglers who are intercepted by agents are attempting to flee and to take bales of drugs back across the border, agents are expected to do what they can to apprehend the suspects and recover the drugs. However, rocks being thrown and the threat of gunfire coming from south of the border create a significant danger justifying defensive action. If agents are only armed with deadly weapons, they are left with few options: retreat, or use their firearms.

  Recommendation: While it is recognized that agents on foot can only carry so many weapons, less lethal weapons should be made available to all agents assigned to high risk areas. PERF's review revealed that in most cases when agents used deadly force, specialized less lethal weapons were not been readily available. In some cases, the use of such less lethal weapons *may* have reduced the risk to agents and prevented the need for deadly force.

  Recommendation: Each field vehicle and boat should be equipped with the best available less lethal weapons, and agents should be required to consider the use of less lethal weapons. In that regard, it should be noted that, in an effort to acquire the best less lethal equipment, CBP now maintains an arsenal that includes a number of different less lethal weapon systems. Consolidation of weapons systems would allow for more uniformity of training and operational capability.

- Personal Protective Equipment (PPE):

  Recommendation: Agents assigned to marine patrol and agents assigned to patrol or who respond near the International Border Fence (IBF) are particularly vulnerable to rock attacks. All agents assigned to these high risk areas should be provided protective equipment to include a helmet with face shield and with integrated communications capability, especially for boat patrol. In addition, all boats and patrol vehicles should be equipped with protective cages/screening.

- Training:

  Recommendation: Policy and skills training is essential to agent safety and appropriate deadly force decisions. Training is especially important to the successful implementation of policy changes. In training, agents should be informed about the reason for changes in policy. For example, with regard to restrictions on shooting at vehicles, it should be explained that shooting at vehicles poses a higher risk to agents and innocent bystanders and should be avoided. If the driver is disabled, the vehicle is likely to continue unguided, creating a different hazard. Agents should receive regular retraining in deadly force policy, use of force decision making, tactical skills and shooting. Command level monitoring of training is particularly important when implementing policy changes where resistance is anticipated.

- Shooting at Vehicles:

  Recommendation: Agents' and the public's safety will be enhanced by policy changes related to shooting at vehicles. CBP should make policy changes that restrict agents from shooting at vehicles. Likewise, agents should be trained to get out of the way of oncoming vehicles as opposed to intentionally assuming a position in the path of such vehicles. The policy should mirror the clear and unambiguous policies that have been in place and which have proven effective in a number of large U.S. jurisdictions for over 40 years. The CBP policy should state **"Agents shall not discharge their firearms at or from a moving vehicle unless deadly physical force is being used against the police officer or another person present, by means other than a moving vehicle."**

- Shooting at Rock Throwers:

  Recommendation: Review of shooting cases involving rock throwers revealed that in some cases agents put themselves in harm's way by remaining in close proximity to the rock throwers when moving out of range was a reasonable option. Too many cases do not appear to meet the test of objective reasonableness with regard to the use of deadly force. In cases where clear options to the use of deadly force exist and are not utilized in rock-throwing incidents, corrective actions should be taken. CBP should improve and refine tactics and policy that focus on operational safety, prioritization of essential activities near the border fence, and use of specialized less lethal weapons with regard to rock throwing incidents. The state CBP policy should be: **"Officers/agents are prohibited from using deadly force against subjects throwing objects not capable of causing serious physical injury or death to them."**

- Public Education / Relations:

    Recommendation: Customs and Border Protection should mount an effort to capture statistical facts regarding incidents and injuries and develop a public education program to inform the residents of risks and potential consequences of such actions related to rock throwing. It is important that the public, especially residents on both sides of the border, and policy makers understand the risk faced by CBP agents and rock throwers along the border. Transparency through timely media releases about attacks and public dialogue regarding border security issues will not end attacks. But when adversarial incidents occur, better public understanding of the issues will provide the agency examples of proactive preventive efforts and put issues in a broader context.

Case Summaries by General Category:

Firearm Use in Response to Armed Suspect Actions
Thirteen such cases were provided.
Observations:

Four of the cases involved CBP agents responding to requests for back-up assistance by local or state law enforcement agencies. Two back-up related shootings were in the State of Maine, one was in California and one was in Texas. Additionally, one CBP shooting took place in Afghanistan. All five of these cases involved confrontations with armed suspects who posed an immediate threat to agents and/or officers.

The eight other firearm to firearm cases involved armed confrontations on or near the Mexican/U.S. Border. All eight of these cases appear to be objectively reasonable and within policy.

Firearm Use in Response to Object Throwing on Water
Four cases involved rocks being thrown at agents who were in boats.
Observations:

It is not clear that all shootings by agents on water to counter rock throwers meet the standard of objective reasonableness. The tactics and strategies that agents are using may unnecessarily put them in harm's way. Moving to a safer location when possible is preferable to using deadly force and such action should be considered as part of objective reasonableness.

Shooting at Vehicles

Fifteen cases were reviewed where shots were fired at or into vehicles by CBP agents.

Observations:

Based on a review of the submitted cases, it appears that CBP practice allows shooting at the driver of any suspect vehicle that comes in the direction of agents. It is suspected that in many vehicle shooting cases, the subject driver was attempting to flee from the agents who intentionally put themselves into the exit path of the vehicle, thereby exposing themselves to additional risk and creating justification for the use of deadly force. In most of these cases, the agents have stated that they were shooting at the driver of a vehicle that was coming at them and posing an imminent threat to their life. In some cases, passengers were struck by agents' gunfire. Little focus has been placed on defensive tactics that could have been used by shooting agents such as getting out of the way. It should be recognized that a ½ ounce (200 grain) bullet is unlikely to stop a 4,000 pound moving vehicle, and if the driver of the approaching vehicle is disabled by a bullet, the vehicle will become a totally unguided threat. Obviously, shooting at a moving vehicle can pose a risk to bystanders including other agents.

The cases suggest that some of the shots at suspect vehicles are taken out of frustration when agents who are on foot have no other way of detaining suspects who are fleeing in a vehicle.

Most reviewed cases involved non-violent suspects who posed no threat other than a moving vehicle.

There is little doubt that the safest course for an agent faced with an oncoming vehicle is to get out of the way of the vehicle.

CBP policy should be "Agents shall not discharge their firearms at or from a moving vehicle unless deadly physical force is being used against the police officer or another person present, by means other than a moving vehicle." Training and policy changes should be implemented to implement this policy.

Shooting At Suspects Throwing Rocks at Agents on Land

Twenty five case files were reviewed that involved shots being fired by agents who had been the victim of rock attacks while on land.

Observations:

Most of the cases involved enforcement activities that took place near the IBF, while a limited number were in remote mountainous regions miles from the border. Some cases seemed to be a clear cut self-defense reaction to close and serious rock threats or assaults, while other shootings were of more questionable justification. The more questionable cases generally involved shootings that took place through the IBF at subjects who were throwing rocks at agents from Mexico. In some cases, agents shot at suspects who were attempting to interfere with arrests on the U.S. side of the border fence. In at least one case, rocks were being thrown in an attempt to allow drugs to be taken back over the IBF. In other cases, agents shot at suspects who started throwing rocks over the fence at them after agents stopped when their CBP vehicles had been hit by rocks. As with vehicle shootings, some cases suggest that frustration is a factor motivating agents to shoot at rock throwers. Likewise, it is felt that some of the weapons discharges are actually intended as warning shots. Two or more shooting cases involving rock throwers on land were ruled by CBP as violations of policy.

It is clear that agents are unnecessarily putting themselves in positions that expose them to higher risk. While rock throwing can result in injuries or death, there must be clear justification to warrant the use of deadly force. CBP needs to train agents to de-escalate these encounters by taking cover, moving out of range and/or using less lethal weapons. Agents should not place themselves into positions where they have no alternative to using deadly force.

Other Shooting Cases

Ten cases that were provided were of a more traditional police shooting nature. They were classified as "other". These shootings were justified by facts ranging from struggles during arrest attempts to an attack by a subject armed with a hammer. Each case was reviewed based on the information that was presented.

Use of Force Policy Review

PERF conducted reviews of the Use of Force Policy Handbook, Office of Training and Development, October 2010 HB 4500-01B, U.S. Customs and Border Protection and

The foreword from the Commissioner represents an opportunity to clearly state the limits on the use of force by Customs and Border Protection officers and agents.

<u>Recommendation:</u> Consideration should be given to adding at the beginning of the foreword a statement similar to the following:

> A *respect* for human life shall guide all members of U.S. Customs and Border Protection in the use of force. CBP officers/agents shall use only the force that is *objectively reasonable* to effectively bring an incident under control, while protecting the life of the officer/agent or others. **Excessive force is strictly prohibited**.

> A Customs and Border Protection officer's/agent's responsibility is the protection of the public. Standards for the use of force are the same on-duty and off-duty. Officers/agents shall not use force that may injure bystanders or hostages, except to preserve life or prevent serious bodily injury. **Deadly force is never justified solely to protect property**. The use of force must be objectively reasonable. The use of force is not left to the unregulated discretion of the involved officer/agent. *Use of force decisions are not driven by the officer/agent, but rather those decisions are dictated by the passive, aggressive, or deadly actions of the resistant or combative subject*. Justification for the use of force is limited to the facts actually known or reasonably perceived by the officer/agent at the moment that force is used. Deadly force shall not be used to effect an arrest or prevent the escape of a person unless that individual presents an imminent threat of death or serious physical injury to officers/agents or others.

> To reiterate, as stated in the Department of Homeland Security Policy on the Use of Deadly Force: "Law enforcement officers and agents of the Department of Homeland Security may use deadly force only when the officer has a reasonable belief that the subject of such force poses an imminent danger of death or serious physical injury to the officer or to another person."

On page 12, C. the Use of Force Policy Division Incident Review Committee is described. Subsection 3 states:
"The UFPD Incident Review Committee shall meet at the discretion of the Director of UFPD, when sufficient use of force data is assembled to warrant the convening of the Committee."

Recommendation: Consideration should be given to having the Incident Review Committee meet on a regular basis, perhaps quarterly, to review current data.

Chapter 4: Use of Force

Section A. General Guidelines describe the circumstances under which force may be used. These standards are those articulated in **Graham v. Connor**, 490 U.S. 386 (1989) decided by the United States Supreme Court.

Recommendation: Consideration should be giving to adding specific reference to *Graham v. Connor*. This will demonstrate that CBP's use of force principles are derived from the highest competent authority, not from internal sources.

Chapter 4: Use of Force, Section C., Subsection 7

Recommendation: Replace the current language with the following.

Officers/agents shall not discharge their firearms at or from a moving vehicle unless deadly physical force is being used against the officer/agent or another person present, by means other than a moving vehicle. (Use of firearms against vessels or aircraft is subject to the restrictions found in 4510-033: Use of Air Disabling Fire Policy.)

A moving vehicle in and of itself is not a presumed threat that justifies the use of deadly force. Firing at or from a moving vehicle is rarely effective and presents extreme danger to agents and innocent persons.

Chapter 4: Use of Force, Section D. Use of Intermediate Force

Recommendation: CBP should consider replacing "Intermediate Force" and "non-deadly" force throughout with "less lethal" which more accurately describe other than deadly force. Consideration should be given to revising Subsection 1 to read: "Less lethal force is defined as that force that in neither likely nor intended to cause death or serious physical injury, although death or serious injury might still be a result."

Chapter 4: Use of Force

Recommendation: Consider adding between Section E. "Emergency Situations" and Section F. "Employee Assistance Program (EAP)" a new section titled "Use of Safe Tactics"

Use of Safe Tactics

1. Vehicle stops (*high risk, low risk, or unknown risk*) present tactical dilemmas for officers/agents. Officers/agents shall not unreasonably place themselves in a position where a threat of imminent danger of death or serious physical injury is created when attempting to stop a motor vehicle or apprehending a felony suspect. When conducting a *high risk stop* or a stop for suspicious circumstances *presenting an unknown risk*, the officer/agent shall employ tactics that promote safety for the officer/agent and the public. This should include utilizing a back-up agent whenever possible.

2. Officers/agents should avoid standing directly in front of, behind, or beside a suspect vehicle and should not intentionally use their body to block the suspect vehicle. The likelihood of injury to the officer/agent substantially increases when using these dangerous and rarely effective tactics. **Officers/agents should strive to move out of the way rather than into the path of vehicles.**

3. Officers/agents will follow all training protocols/guidelines which are taught in entry level training relative to *high risk stops* involving vehicles and armed suspects.

4. CBP recognizes that the mobility of vehicles present heightened risks for officers/agents and discourages officers from reaching into vehicles. This tactic is extremely dangerous and rarely effective.

5. Thrown or hurled missiles aimed at officers/agents may represent a threat of imminent danger of death or serious physical injury. When sufficient time exists officers/agents should seek cover and/or move out of range. Such action may be especially viable when the attack is coming from the other side of the border. *Officers/agents are prohibited from using deadly force against subjects throwing objects not capable of causing serious physical injury or death to them.*

Chapter 4: Use of Force, Section F. Employee Assistance Program (EAP), Section 3 states:

3. When an Authorized Officer/Agent uses deadly force, either on or off-duty, *which results in death or serious physical injury to a person*, the officer/agent shall (after providing incident information in accordance with the requirements of Chapter 5.A.2.d.(1-8)) be placed on Administrative Leave with pay and/or regularly scheduled days off for three (3) consecutive calendar days. During this period, the officer/agent may voluntarily participate in a confidential consultation conducted by an EAP counselor. The RO, on a case-by-case basis, shall grant requests for additional administrative leave for the confidential consultation or other related purposes. {Italics added}

Recommendation: Consideration should be given to removing the following: "*which results in death or serious physical injury to a person.*" All policies related to the use of deadly force should be neutral with regard to the outcome. The issue is one of intent. The behavior of the officer/agent should be dealt with regardless of the impact of the use of deadly force on a suspect.

Recommendation: Consultation with an EAP counselor should be mandatory. This will remove any stigma some may feel is associated with counseling sessions.

Chapter 5: Use of Force Reporting Requirements, Section A. 2. c. states:

c. Any Authorized Officer/Agent who participates in or observes *a reportable use of deadly force incident* shall orally report the incident to a supervisor in accordance with the requirements of this chapter. {Italics added.}

Recommendation: The term "reportable use of deadly force" implies that there are non-reportable uses of deadly force. Consideration should be given to eliminating "reportable" wherever it is used in a like manner.

Chapter 5: Use of Force Reporting Requirements, Section A. 5. a. states:

a. In any use of force incident where there is a death or serious injury as a result of actions taken by a CBP Officer, Agent or employee, the RO shall ensure that the incident has been reported to the law enforcement authorities having jurisdiction over the investigation.

Recommendation: Consideration should be given to expanding the notification requirement to include not only incidents where there is a death or serious injury but also whenever there is a use of deadly force. This will cover both less lethal incidents – when death or serious injury results -- and use of deadly force incidents. The current notification requirement does not cover, for example, an episode during which multiple shots are fired but no one is hit.

Chapter 5: Use of Force Reporting Requirements, Section B: Investigation of Reportable Use of Deadly Force and Section C: Incident Investigation

Best practice in U.S. policing is that all use of deadly force incidents undergo a dual investigation. One investigation is to determine whether any criminal charges are warranted. The second investigation is to determine whether the agency's rules, regulations, policies or procedures were breached. The second investigation, an administrative, internal investigation, must be consistent with Garrity v. New Jersey, 385 U.S. 493 (1966). The Garrity rule requires that information received in an administrative investigation cannot be used in the criminal investigation. (However, information from the criminal investigation can be used in the administrative investigation.)

Section B appears to provide guidelines for criminal investigations of incidents involving the use of deadly force by CBP officers/agents while Section C appears to provide guidance for the administrative investigation.

Recommendation: Consideration should be given to changing the title of Chapter 5 from "Use of Force Reporting Requirements" to "Use of Force Reporting and Investigation Requirements" to more accurately reflect the content of the chapter.

Recommendation: The chapter should specifically describe that dual investigations will occur and appropriately label the sections that pertain to criminal investigations and administrative investigations.

Recommendation: Customs and Border Protection has no criminal investigative arm. Hence it is dependent on local law enforcement agencies when they have primary jurisdiction, or elements of DOJ or DHS/CBP if DOJ or DHS/CBP has primary jurisdiction, to conduct criminal investigations. To ensure that criminal investigations of the use of deadly force by CBP officers/agents are conducted consistently on a timely basis, CBP should strive to identify a single federal source for all criminal investigations of deadly force incidents. This recommendation is not intended to preclude criminal investigations by local authorities, a dual investigation could occur.

There should be clear guidelines to foster close coordination among investigating agencies so there is no confusion which agency has primary investigative jurisdiction. Protocols should b established in advance of incidents.

Chapter 5: Use of Force Reporting Requirements

Recommendation: In Section A, 4, c reference is made to a Critical Incident Team (CIT) that may initiate a parallel investigation into an incident. There is no other definition or description of a CIT. Such information should be added to the Handbook.

Chapter 5: Use of Force Reporting Requirements, Section D: CBP Personnel Involved in a Use of Deadly Force Incident, Subsection 2 states:

2. CBP's Drug-Free Federal Workplace Program – Post-incident drug testing shall be required when there is a reasonable suspicion that the actions of the officer/agent were the result of illegal drug use. The decision to require post-incident testing must be based on articulable facts, evidence and circumstances and be undertaken in accordance with the standards and procedures documented in Chapter 5, Part C of the *U.S. Customs Service Drug-Free Federal Workplace Program* (CIS HB 51200-01A), dated April 2002.

Recommendation: Consideration should be given to revising the subsection to require post-incident drug **and alcohol** testing after every Use of Deadly Force Incident. The CBP should hold its officers/agents strictly accountable to be unimpaired in their work. This is especially important with regard to the use of deadly force.

Chapter 5: Use of Force Reporting Requirements, E. Discharge of a Firearm

Recommendation: The directive seems to equate "Discharge of a Firearm" with "Use of Deadly Force." While every Use of Deadly Force Incident should be reportable, some firearms discharges can be excepted as described elsewhere in Chapter 5.E.

Chapter 5: Use of Force Reporting Requirements, E. Discharge of a Firearm, Subsection a.(2)

(2) While off duty, and causes any injury to any person, or any damage to either private, public, or government property in violation of any law or ordinance, or causes an investigation by any law enforcement agency;

Recommendation: The subsection should be altered so that all off duty firearms discharges, except those that occur during sanctioned off duty practice, are reportable regardless of location or outcome.

Chapter 5: Use of Force Reporting Requirements, Subsection 2

2. After any discharge resulting in personal injury or property damage where a firearm malfunction is suspected, the RO must immediately send the firearm and ammunition to the appropriate UFPD facility for examination, unless the firearm is required for an ongoing federal, state or local law enforcement investigation or legal action.

Recommendation: Consider altering the section so that any discharge where a firearm malfunction is suspected results in sending the firearm and ammunition to the appropriate UFPD facility for examination. Every weapon always should be maintained in good working order. Each suspected malfunction should be examined, not only those where the discharge results in personal injury or property damage.

Chapter 6: Use of Force Proficiency and Training

The requirement that officers/agents demonstrate their firearms proficiency quarterly represents a law enforcement best practice.

Recommendation: At least one of the quarterly firearms proficiency sessions should include judgment shooting. This may include computer based scenarios, simunitions or similar training to place officers/agents in situations where they need to decide whether to shoot as well as to demonstrate accuracy. Some of these sessions should include scenarios where use of less lethal weapons might be an option; when taking covering or moving out of range is the best option; and when de-escalation tactics can prove to be successful.

Chapter 6: Use of Force Proficiency and Training, D. Firearms Instructors, Subsection 5 states that:

5. FIs are required to be re-certified at least once every five (5) years through a re-certification program approved by the Director of UFPD. On a case-by-case basis, an extension of one (1) year may be approved by the Director of UFPD.

Recommendation: Consideration should be given to requiring all firearms instructors to complete an annual training update. Such updates could be delivered electronically and could cover changes in firearms technology, ammunition and tactics.

Chapter 6: Use of Force Proficiency and Training, Section F. Intermediate Use of Force Proficiency and Training

Recommendation: Beginning here and throughout this chapter ,consideration should be given to changing "intermediate force" to "less lethal force" and "intermediate force devices" to "less lethal weapons." By making these changes, CBP will acknowledge the gravity that characterizes the entire spectrum of use of force techniques and equipment by law enforcement agencies.

Chapter 6: Use of Force Proficiency and Training, J. Intermediate Force Instructors (IFIs) & Intermediate Force Instructor Trainers

IFIs are required to be re-certified at least once every five (5) years.

Recommendation: Consideration should be given to establishing the re-certification requirement for less lethal instructors to every three years. The technology and tactics pertinent to less lethal weapons is continuing to evolve and at a faster rate than with firearms. Decreasing the time until recertification for less lethal instructors will help keep them up-to-date with new less lethal weapons and use guidelines. As with firearms instructors, consideration should be given to implementing an annual refresher process.

Chapter 7: Intermediate Force Devices

Recommendation: Consideration should be giving to changing the language from Intermediate Force Devices to Less Lethal Weapons.

Recommendation: There is no reference in the chapter to Electronic Control Weapons. Revisions to this chapter should be made to include references and discussion about Electronic Control Weapons.

Appendix IV CBP – Authorized Firearms and Intermediate Force Devices

Recommendation: Consideration should be giving to changing the langrage from Intermediate Force Devices to Less Lethal Weapons.

Recommendation: Consideration should be given to revisions in this Appendix to include references to Electronic Control Weapons.

Recommendation: CBP authorizes a variety of launchers designed to stun, deliver a chemical irritant and/or kinetic impact projectile without causing serious physical injury of death.. Consideration should be given to reducing the number to one after research and review. This will allow greater standardization of training and reduce confusion about which weapon to use.

Appendix V. CBP Use of Force Continuum

Recommendation: Reference to the requirements of *Graham v Connor* should be added as part of introduction.

Recommendation: Information about Electronic Control Weapons should be added.

Appendix VI CBP Form 318

Recommendation: The form should be revised to include references to Electronic Control Weapons as appropriate.

4510-020C: U.S. CUSTOMS AND BORDER PROTECTION BODY ARMOR POLICY

Section 7 BODY ARMOR WEAR

Subsection 7.1 states in part: "The wearing of body armor during normal operations is at the discretion of the employee."

Recommendation: Consideration should be given to mandatory wearing of body armor. In a recent PERF survey of U.S. police officers (2011), respondents identified a variety of situations in which body armor prevented or mitigated injuries including gun shots, car accidents, knife or edged weapon assaults and punches, kicks or other strikes.

Recommendation: Consideration should be given to the development of protective head gear for all CBP officers/agents. Such protection has the potential to reduce the danger of head injuries from thrown projectiles. CBP should consider developing specifications that would result in head gear that offers protection, has communication capabilities, and is suitable for the variety of conditions and climates in which CBP officer/agents work.

4510-026B: CONTROLLED TIRE DEFLATION DEVICE DIRECTIVE

No recommendations.

4510-029 PEPPERBALL LAUCHING SYSTEM (PLS) POLICY

Section 5.6 Intermediate Force

Recommendation: Consideration should be given to changing the language from Intermediate Force to Less Lethal Force both here and throughout the policy.

Section 6.1 PLS – TRAINING GUIDELINES, Subsection 6.1.5 states:
"Participation in the training and certification for the PLS shall be voluntary."

Recommendation: If there is a desire to expand the use of less lethal weapons, consideration should be given to making PLS training and certification mandatory for all officers/agents.

4510-029A: USE OF ELECTONIC CONTROL DEVICES

Recommendation: Consideration should be given to using the more contemporary language of Electronic Control Weapons (ECWs). This enhances the recognition of the danger in using these tools.

Recommendation: Consideration should be given to replacing "intermediate force" with "less lethal force."

Section 6.1 POLICY – TRAINING GUIDELINES, Subsection 6.1.3 states:
"Participation in the training and certification of ECD end users/operators shall be voluntary."

Recommendation: If there is a desire to expand the use of less lethal weapons consideration should be given to making ECW training and certification mandatory for all officers/agents.

Section 6.2 POLICY – OPERATIONAL GUIDELINES

Recommendation: Consideration should be given to replacing Subsection 6.2.4 which now reads:
"Subject to the exceptions described in 6.2.5 below, an ECD may be utilized as a compliance tool on a subject offering, at a minimum, active resistance."

The following replacement language is adapted from the guidelines for "Using the ECW" found in "2011 Electronic Control Weapon Guidelines" published by the Police Executive Research Forum and the U.S. Department of Justice, Community Oriented Policing Services, page 20, number 25. This replacement guideline should be as follows:

"ECWs should be used only against subjects who are exhibiting active resistance in a manner that, in the agent's judgment, is likely to result in injuries to themselves or others. ECWs should not be used against a passive subject."

This will clarify the restrictions on ECW use.

Recommendation: Consideration should be given to replacing Subsection 6.2.6.

Subsection 6.2.6 now reads: "A subject should not receive more that three (3) ECD cycles. Each ECD cycle must be reasonable and necessary to overcome non-compliance by an actively resistant subject and to accomplish the officer/agent's legitimate law enforcement duties. If the use of the ECD is unsuccessful, the officer/agent should transition to another reasonable force option."

The following replacement language is adapted from the guidelines for "Using the ECW" found in "2011 Electronic Control Weapon Guidelines" published by the Police Executive Research Forum and the U.S. Department of Justice, Community Oriented Policing Services, page 20, number 21. **The current language should be replaced by the following guideline:**

"Personnel should use an ECW for one standard cycle (five seconds) and then evaluate the situation to determine if subsequent cycles are necessary. Each ECW cycle must be reasonable and necessary to overcome non-compliance by an actively resistant subject and to accomplish the officer/agent's legitimate law enforcement duties. Personnel should consider that exposure to the ECW for longer than 15 seconds (whether due to multiple applications or continuous cycling) may increase the risk of death or serious injury. Any subsequent applications should be independently justifiable, and the risks should be weighed against other force options."

This change will bring the CBP guideline to the level of best practice and provide additional cautionary information.

Recommendation: the following subsection should be added. It is absent from the directive.

"Personnel should not intentionally activate more than one ECW at a time against a subject."

Recommendation: To comply with best practice as specified in "Using the ECW" found in "2011 Electronic Control Weapon Guidelines" published by the Police Executive Research Forum and the U.S. Department of Justice, Community Oriented Policing Services, page 20, number 26 the following subsection should be added:

"Fleeing should not be the sole justification for using an ECW against a subject. Agents should consider the severity of the offense, the subject's threat level to others, and the risk of serious injury to the subject before deciding to use an ECW on a fleeing subject."

4510-031: FN303 LESS LETHAL LAUNCHER SYSTEM POLICY

Section 6.1 POLICY – TRAINING GUIDELINES, Subsection 6.1.3 states:
"Participation in the training and certification for the FN303 shall be voluntary"

Recommendation: If there is a desire to expand the use of less lethal weapons, consideration should be given to making FN303 training and certification mandatory for all officers/agents.

Recommendation: Replace "intermediate force" throughout with "less lethal force."

4510-032: LESS LETHAL SPECIALTY IMPACT – CHEMICAL MUNTIONS POLICY

Section 6.1 POLICY – TRAINING GUIDELINES, Subsection 6.1.3 states:
"Participation in the training and certification for the LLSI-CM systems shall be voluntary."

Recommendation: If there is a desire to expand the use of less lethal weapons, consideration should be given to making LLSI-CM systems training and certification mandatory for all officers/agents.

4510-033: USE OF AIR DISABLING FIRE POLICY

Section 8.2 Air Disabling Fire (ADFR) REPORTING PROCEDURES, Subsection 8.6 states that:
Any use of an ADFR that results in serious physical injury or death shall follow CBP policy and procedures for reporting and responding to the use of deadly force.

Recommendation: Consideration should be given to requiring all ADFR utilization to follow Use of Deadly Force reporting and investigation guidelines. Regardless of the outcome, all ADFR use should be subject to systematic inquiry to assess whether current training and tactics are followed.

4510-034: CBP USE OF FORCE STEERING COMMITTEE (UFSC)

No recommendations.

4510-035: FOREIGN ATTACHÉ FIREARMS DIRECTIVE

No recommendations for change.

5290-012A: CBP USE OF FORCE INCIDENT REVIEW PROGRAM

1. PURPOSE The statement describing the purpose of the program is stated as follows:
"The U.S. Customs and Border Protection (CBP) CBP Use of Force Incident Review Program is designed to promote the safety of CBP law enforcement personnel and enhance existing training, tactics, equipment and policy."

Recommendation: Consideration should be given to expanding the purpose of the review program to include "preserving the life and reducing injuries of all those whose actions necessitate the use of force directed at them by CBP law enforcement personnel."

Use of force reviews should serve a dual purpose, enhancing the safety of law enforcement officers and the safety of those they come into contact with.